QUEEN VICTORIA

FRONT COVER: *State portrait of Queen Victoria in 1859. The German court artist Franz Winterhalter catches the regal opulence of the Queen's middle years. Barry's new Palace of Westminster appears in the background.*

BACK COVER: *The Widow of Windsor. Queen Victoria in 1875, painted by Joachim von Angeli. Splendour has been put aside, but the controlled severity of widowhood is if anything more impressive.*

FACING PAGE: *One of the last photographs taken of Victoria and Albert together* (c. 1860). ABOVE: *Stately domesticity (Winterhalter, 1846). The Prince of Wales is beside the Queen; Princess Helena had been born in May.*

QUEEN VICTORIA

Michael St John Parker

KING GEORGE III had a large family—fifteen sons and daughters in all. But this plentiful brood failed to provide him with legitimate grandchildren who could succeed to the throne. His eldest son, George, who acted as Prince Regent during the periods of derangement which afflicted the old king in his later years, had only one child, a daughter who died in childbirth in 1817 together with her infant son. Of the Regent's surviving brothers and sisters at that time, not one could boast a regular heir.

The looming succession crisis was further complicated by the fact that the royal family occupied a deplorably low place in the public esteem at this period. The poor, mad king himself was an object of respectful pity; but his numerous offspring were felt to have little to recommend them, and the men in particular had contrived to make themselves positively unacceptable even to that easy-going age. The Prince Regent was shortly to divorce his wife amid unparalleled public scandal; the Duke of Cumberland was suspected of being a murderer, among other things; and of the Dukes of Clarence and Kent, the great Wellington exploded indignantly "They are the greatest millstones about the necks of any government that can be imagined. They have insulted—*personally* insulted—two thirds of the gentlemen of England!" The debts of these royal ne'er-do-wells were so enormous that Parliament, to its great disgust, was recurrently called upon to increase their already substantial allowances. With his usual trenchant precision, Wellington had put his finger on the most sensitive part of the problem. The Crown still had great importance in the political life of the country, but its survival depended on the goodwill of the classes who effectively dominated Parliament and the counties. This goodwill was seriously endangered in the early nineteenth century, and it was to be a significant part of Queen Victoria's claim to greatness that she rescued the royal family from disrepute and gave it a new place in a changing world. She

'. . . kept her throne unshaken still,
Broad based upon the people's will.'

It is not likely, however, that such grand ideas occurred to the royal dukes when, in 1817, they realised that unless one of them produced a child reasonably soon, the succession to the throne would be in doubt. Once this fact was apparent, there was a rush to provide the essential heir. The effective winner was Edward, Duke of Kent. A bluff martinet of a man, plagued like his brothers by overwhelming debts, he married the widowed Princess Victoria of Saxe-Coburg in 1818, and the result was a daughter, Princess Victoria, born on 24 May 1819 in Kensington Palace.

The place of birth itself owed something to good luck. The Duke of Kent had gone to live for economy's sake on his wife's German estate, but was determined that his child should be born at home in England—partly at least because, a long time before, a gypsy had prophesied that he would become the father of a great queen, who must, of course, be born on English soil. So the ducal couple had set off across northern Europe at an advanced stage of the Duchess's pregnancy, with all their personal belongings piled into an enormous shabby coach driven for want of a coachman by the Duke himself. "An unbelievably odd caravan", commented one observer. However, they arrived safely at Dover, a month before the confinement.

The Duke was delighted; but he did not live long to enjoy his success. A cold caught in Salisbury Cathedral worsened to a fatal congestion and in his home at Sidmouth he died on 23 January 1820, six days before his father, George III. His little child was left to be brought up by a mother who hardly spoke English, in conditions of relative poverty (judged, at least, by the royal standards of that time), among hostile and indifferent relations.

It is not surprising, then, that Princess Victoria's childhood was on the whole quiet and almost simple.

Continued on page 6

*

FACING PAGE: *The Duke of Kent, fourth son of George III, and father of Victoria. In 1802, the year of this portrait, he became Governor of Gibraltar, where his severity caused a series of mutinies.*
ABOVE: *The Duchess of Kent with Princess Victoria in 1834. After her husband's death the Duchess worked hard to secure her daughter's place near the throne.*
RIGHT: *Baroness Lehzen, Victoria's devoted if demanding governess. She did much to form the character of the young princess.*

3

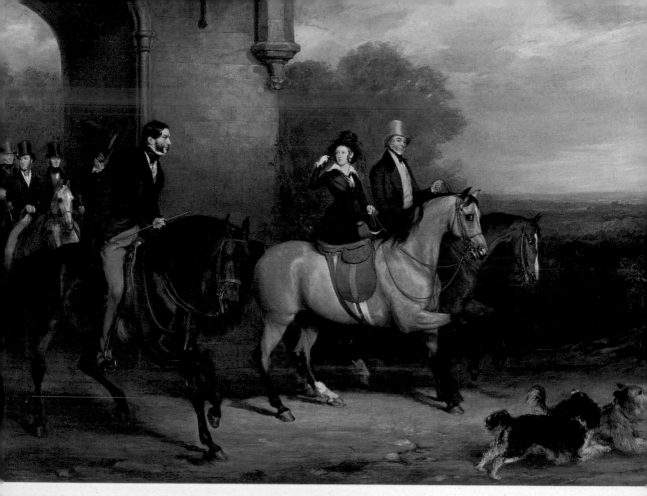

This group of pictures captures the freshness of the early morning of Victoria's reign.

ABOVE: The young Queen rides out with Lord Melbourne, the minister whose shrewdly benign advice did much to shape her early political awareness, and to whose warm devotion she responded with eager affection.

LEFT: 20 June 1837. The famous dawn scene at Kensington Palace, when Lord Conyngham (the Lord Chamberlain) and Archbishop Howley of Canterbury bring the news of William IV's death and Victoria's accession. The flavour of the eighteenth century is still strong in this idealised midsummer awakening.

FACING PAGE: The Coronation, 28 June 1838, in Westminster Abbey. The falling sunbeams were noticed by contemporary observers, who saw in them symbolic significance. The artist has depicted an episode in the homage of the peers, when the aged Lord Rolle tripped and fell, but struggled forward—whereat the Queen rose from her throne to meet him, amid sympathetic applause.

She saw little of her eldest uncle, now King George IV, though when they did meet she seemed to know how to please him. There is a delightful account of a visit to Windsor in 1826; a band was playing in a barge on Virginia Water, and the little princess was asked what she would like them to perform next: "Oh, Uncle King," came the swift reply, "I should like them to play 'God Save The King'!"

At this stage, however, Victoria was not aware how close she herself stood to the throne. This realisation came—or was prompted—in March of 1830, and had a sobering effect; a burst of tears, followed by the famous promise, "I will be good", suggest fairly enough the highly-strung, conscientious temperament that was to distinguish Victoria throughout her life.

The governess who engineered this revelation, Baroness Lehzen, was doubtless aware that the Princess was about to be brought significantly nearer to her destiny. The first of the two uncles who stood between Victoria and the throne was already dying, and was succeeded in June 1830 by his younger brother the Duke of Clarence, who became William IV. The new king was a colourful and short-tempered eccentric, whose lack of tact was matched by his lack of brains. Never an easy man to deal with, he encountered in Victoria's mother, the Duchess of Kent, an opponent whose stubborn assertiveness frequently rendered him almost apoplectic with fury.

The duchess was a vigorous and emotional woman, devoted to her daughter and determined to assert the rights of the heir apparent to the throne. Her own standing, however, was precarious, and her well-meant efforts on her daughter's behalf had a mixed success. The king was enraged by elaborately stage-managed 'progresses', on which the Princess Victoria was received with the crash of saluting guns; and the princess herself found her mother's care over-possessive, so that at the first opportunity—in fact, on the day she became Queen—she broke away, and relegated the duchess to the background. Not until much later in life did mother and daughter come together again, and it was only after the Duchess's death in 1861 that Victoria, reading through her mother's letters and journals, became fully aware of the extent of her loving care. The realisation brought overwhelming grief, and something like a nervous breakdown.

It was, then, a difficult background against which this sensitive, perceptive child had to grow up. Squabbling servants and feuding factions, jockeying for position as the old king declined, added to the complications of life, and when William IV eventually died it is not surprising to find the new Queen asserting her naturally strong will with capricious and even frivolous emphasis.

Kensington Palace was still sleeping in the idyllic midsummer dawn when the Archbishop of Canterbury and the Lord Chamberlain arrived at 5.00 a.m. on 20 June 1837 to announce to the Princess that she was now Queen. And indeed the whole of the early part of the new reign had a dawn-like quality about it. The innocent glamour

Continued on page 8

Politics and government—the early years.

FACING PAGE: *the two great Tory statesmen during the first part of the reign were the Duke of Wellington and Sir Robert Peel, pictured here together by Winterhalter. The Iron Duke (left) was universally respected, not least by Victoria. Peel, on the other hand, stood for a long while outside her favour; she found him "such a cold, odd man" by contrast with his political opponent and her favourite, Lord Melbourne.*

ABOVE: *Sir David Wilkie's painting commemorating Victoria's first Council drew the Queen's praise in 1837—she thought all the likenesses were excellent. Ten years later her opinion had altered —she decided it was one of the worst she had ever seen.*

RIGHT: *Chartism was regarded by some contemporaries as a herald of revolution. But the climax of the movement, a great rally held at Kennington Common (10 April 1848), fizzled out in rain and respectability. Victorian England was too strong to be shaken by such political eccentricities.*

THE CHARTIST DEMONSTRATION ON KENNINGTON COMMON.

of the young sovereign—her beautiful poise, the elegance of her movements, the mingled charm and dignity of her presence, her captivating silvery laugh —everything about her entranced all who met her, and roused a glow of chivalrous loyalty among innumerable subjects who only heard about her, but to whom she was a fairy-tale monarch come true.

Needless to say, such an idyll could not last, and to school her in the harsh world of real public life she was immeasurably fortunate in finding as her Prime Minister the most perfect of tutors—Lord Melbourne. Shrewd, kindly, amusing, infinitely civilised, he was a complete Whig aristocrat and a perfect man of the world. "He has such *stores* of knowledge; such a wonderful memory; he knows about everything and everybody; *who* they were and *what* they did; and he im-

parts all his knowledge in such a *kind* and agreeable manner; it does me a *world* of good; and his conversations always *improve* one greatly."

His influence was great not merely because he supplied wise guidance at a critical moment, acting as the ideal uncle, but also because both he and Queen Victoria had certain important traits in common—an instinct for people rather than systems, an attachment to realistic commonsense, a hearty enjoyment of life. In other respects they differed sharply, and in due course the other facets of the Queen's character were to be worked on and brought to the fore by the very different influence of Prince Albert. But the qualities shared with Melbourne remained unimpaired through a long life, and provided a large part of the secret of the Queen's success as a ruler.

The depth of her attachment to Melbourne proved a liability, however, in 1839 when it betrayed her into an imprudent and almost unconstitutional support for the political party which he headed, at a time when its command of the House of Commons was faltering. The Bedchamber Crisis (so-called because it revolved around the issue of appointments in the royal household) was resolved by the tact and loyalty of the statesmen concerned, but evidently the Queen needed an emotional focus that would not involve her in the manoeuvrings of politicians. This was supplied by her marriage to Albert, Prince of Saxe-Coburg-Gotha.

Prince Albert had been marked out as a possible consort for some time, at least by such subtle intriguers as the Queen's relative, King Leopold of Belgium and his adviser, Baron Stock-

Continued on page 11

FACING PAGE: *Royal weddings in the nineteenth century were not the great public occasions that they have since become. Queen Victoria married Prince Albert in the Chapel Royal of St. James's Palace, on 10 February 1840, before a small congregation of relatives and notabilities. Sir George Hayter's stiffly-posed commemoration of the scene shows the young couple surrounded by their families—Victoria's mother, the Duchess of Kent, her uncles the Dukes of Sussex (in black skull-cap) and Cambridge, her aunt, Queen Adelaide (widow of William IV), and Albert's brother Ernest, Duke of Saxe-Coburg-Gotha. Lord Melbourne carries the sword of state.*

RIGHT: *Court painters commonly idealise their subjects, but Victoria's beloved Albert really was the exemplary martial figure, administrator, and cultured prince celebrated here by Winterhalter; our eyes may also find him rather stiff and dull.*

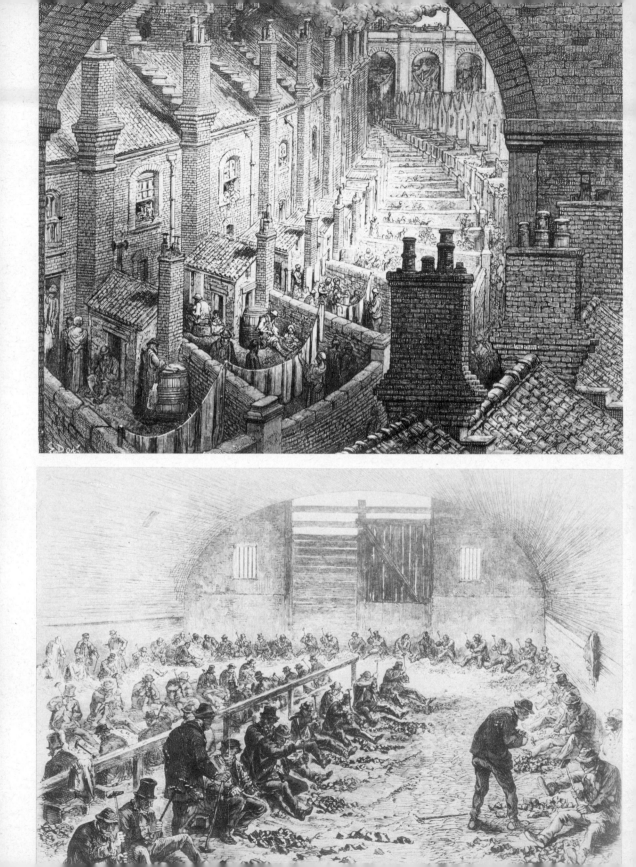

mar. It was thus, in a sense, an arranged match; but Queen Victoria was very much her own mistress, and not at all inclined to accept any candidate for her hand simply because he was considered suitable by other people. She was contemplating marriage, though with doubt and uncertainty, from early 1839; but when Prince Albert visited Windsor later in the year the matter suddenly settled itself. She had met him once before, but that had been an insignificant

*

FACING PAGE: *A contrast to splendour. (Above) the engravings of the French artist Gustave Doré illuminate with a weird and sinister light the nightmare social conditions that prevailed among so many of Victoria's subjects. (Below) unemployed men breaking stones in Bethnal Green, c. 1860s.*

ABOVE: *Lord John Russell* (left) *and Lord Palmerston* (right), *the two great Whig statesmen of the mid-nineteenth century; Queen Victoria called them "the two dreadful old men". Russell was a prime mover in the great Reform Bills of 1832 and 1867, and Palmerston's diplomacy frequently set Europe by the ears. A third aristocratic statesman, Lord Salisbury* (centre), *dominated politics during the last part of the Queen's reign; his 13½ years as Prime Minister at the head of the Conservative party saw the Palmerstonian tradition of jingoism turned into a more grandiose style—imperialism.*

encounter; now, at 7.30 on the evening of 10 October, as she stood at the top of the torchlit castle steps to greet the pale young man in black travelling clothes, she fell in love. Her journal records the event—"It was with some emotion that I beheld Albert—who is *beautiful*"!

Hesitation followed by swift and imperious decision was characteristic of the Queen throughout her life, and never more so than on this occasion. Four days after Albert's arrival, she was discussing arrangements with Lord Melbourne, including the awkwardness of having to take the initiative, as she must by virtue of her position. On 15 October she asked Albert to marry her. "I told him I was quite unworthy of him. He said he would be very happy to spend his life with me. I *love* him more than I can say, and I shall do everything in my power to render the sacrifice he has made (for sacrifice in my opinion it is) as small as I can."

An ecstatic love affair was rapidly transformed into a devoted marriage. The wedding took place on 10 February 1840, in the Chapel Royal of St. James's Palace. In a brief moment of privacy afterwards, snatched from the crowded ceremonies of the day, husband and wife promised each other that there must never be an unshared secret; more than twenty years later, a desolate widow noted "There never was".

The Prince Consort (a title that he was not formally granted until 1857)

was never popular in England. He rode and shot, fenced and danced superbly; he was highly intelligent, widely travelled and well read; he was a conscientious and unremitting worker, and his judgement was at least as sound as that of most English politicians; he was a man of the highest integrity and principle. But he lacked ease and confidence, as is the way of a man who makes duty do service for vitality; he never quite fitted into any section of English society; as the Queen's foreign husband, his position was always ambiguous and often suspect; in the end, perhaps, the cynical English just found him too good to be true.

There was an irony in the nation's refusal to accept Prince Albert, since the virtues that characterised this admirable man were also, in very large measure, those of the age which we call "Victorian". But in the Queen's adoring eyes, the Prince's unpopularity was an offence and a source of resentment, and although herself of a far more robust temperament than her husband, she allowed loyalty to him to cloud her relationship with her people, both during their marriage and, still more, after his death.

She allowed him, also, to effect something of a transformation in herself. By nature a dutiful person, she willingly learnt from him habits of methodical application and sober routine. The patterns of activity which resulted were to become increasingly important as the monarchy evolved

Continued on page 14

Queen Victoria and her family

By 1887, the year of her Golden Jubilee, Queen Victoria was a matriarch among the kings and princes of Europe. The connections inherited from her German ancestry had been multiplied by the marriages of her own children and grandchildren, and personal influence (though she used it sparingly) was thus added to her prestige as ruler of the greatest Empire the world had ever seen. The Jubilee itself was both a great celebration of the Imperial ideal and a stimulus to further advance. This painting by L. Tuxen which commemorates the event, shows Her Majesty the Queen surrounded by members of the Royal Family.

1 Her Majesty The Queen
2 The Prince of Wales
3 The Princess of Wales
4 Prince Albert Victor
5 Prince George of Wales
6 Princess Louise of Wales
7 Princess Victoria of Wales
8 Princess Maud of Wales
9 Crown Princess of Germany
10 Crown Prince of Germany
11 Prince William of Prussia
12 Princess William of Prussia
13 Prince Frederick William of Prussia
14 The Hereditary Princess of Saxe-Meiningen
15 The Hereditary Prince of Saxe-Meiningen
16 Princess Theodore of Saxe-Meiningen
17 Prince Henry of Prussia
18 Princess Irene of Hesse
19 Princess Victoria of Prussia
20 Princess Sophie of Prussia
21 Princess Margaret of Prussia
22 The Grand Duke of Hesse
23 Princess Louis of Battenberg
24 Prince Louis of Battenberg
25 Princess Alice of Battenberg
26 The Grand Duchess Elizabeth of Russia
27 The Grand Duke Serge of Russia
28 The Hereditary Grand Duke of Hesse
29 Princess Alix of Hesse
30 The Duke of Edinburgh
31 The Duchess of Edinburgh
32 Prince Alfred of Edinburgh
33 Princess Marie of Edinburgh
34 Princess Victoria Melita of Edinburgh
35 Princess Alexandra of Edinburgh
36 Princess Beatrice of Edinburgh
37 Princess Christian of Schleswig-Holstein, Princess Helena of Great Britain and Ireland
38 Prince Christian of Schleswig-Holstein
39 Prince Christian Victor of Schleswig-Holstein
40 Prince Albert of Schleswig-Holstein
41 Princess Victoria of Schleswig-Holstein
42 Princess Louise of Schleswig-Holstein
43 Princess Louise, Marchioness of Lorne
44 The Marquess of Lorne
45 The Duke of Connaught
46 The Duchess of Connaught
47 Princess Margaret of Connaught
48 Prince Arthur of Connaught
49 Princess Victoria Beatrice Patricia of Connaught
50 The Duchess of Albany
51 Princess Alice of Albany
52 Prince Charles Edward, Duke of Albany
53 Princess Beatrice, Princess Henry of Battenberg
54 Prince Henry of Battenberg
55 Prince Alexander Albert of Battenberg

from its eighteenth-century role of active participation in government to its more modern function as Head of State. Queen Victoria's long reign saw the critical stages of this evolutionary process, and while Prince Albert was alive the royal couple's conception of their duty tended to involve them rather positively in the business of government. When she was left to herself in widowhood, the Queen's natural realism and distrust of systems inclined her to wait on events in a way that was probably better fitted in the long run to the part that the Crown was coming to play.

The most important example of the strains that arose from an 'active' approach to the duties of the Crown was the long and bitter struggle with Lord Palmerston. This jaunty, devil-may-care patriot, with his Regency manners and morals, may have been the idol of the public, but he could not possibly attract the esteem of the royal couple, to whom in fact he behaved with almost unconstitutional disrespect. "The levity of the man is almost inconceivable", exclaimed the Queen in bitter complaint, and she and her husband in their turn went

close to the limits of constitutional propriety in trying to rid themselves of a minister whom they considered a political disaster as well as a personal menace. There was a good deal to be said on both sides of the argument; but it is generally agreed that Prince Albert's last contribution, when he revised the draft of a message composed by Palmerston and Lord John Russell, the Prime Minister, immediately before retiring to his deathbed in December 1861, saved England from a certain crisis and possible war with the Federal States of America.

A happier episode, and the peak of the Prince's success in England, was the great Exhibition of 1851 which was held in Hyde Park. This celebration of the nation's industrial and commercial greatness was very largely Prince Albert's own conception. The dazzling and epoch-making engineering masterpiece in which it was staged was the result of his own imaginative patronage; the immense and meticulous organisation was carried out entirely under his personal and detailed direction; and the whole affair was a brilliant and unqualified success. The huge 'Crystal Palace' was visited

by more than six million people between May and October, and made a profit of £186,000. With its avowed object of the bettering of mankind, the Great Exhibition may stand as the supreme example of that new involvement in practical affairs and social responsibility which Prince Albert taught Queen Victoria to regard as one of the main functions of monarchy in the modern age.

*

Animals, domestic informality, the Scottish Highlands—all of Sir Edwin Landseer's favourite subjects as a painter were such as to endear him to Queen Victoria. ABOVE: *the young Queen, the Prince Consort and the Princess Royal at Windsor.* FACING PAGE, above: *the Queen at Loch Muick in 1850. This type of picture, showing the monarch at ease among her subjects, marked a new departure, as Victoria was well aware: "It is quite a new conception; it will tell a great deal."* FACING PAGE, below: *Queen Victoria at Osborne; the attendant is John Brown.*

Continued on page 17

The Great Exhibition

The Crystal Palace Exhibition of 1851, celebrating the triumph of peace and progress through science, trade and industry, was a symbolic demonstration of Britain's short-lived supremacy as the 'Workshop of the World'. It was also a brilliant personal success for Prince Albert, its originator and organiser. Paxton's masterpiece of engineering architecture attracted vast crowds, including the fashionable world who had sneered at the project in its early stages.

'As though 'twere by a wizard's rod
A blazing arch of lucid glass
Leaps like a fountain from the grass
To meet the sun.'

ABOVE: View of the south side. LEFT: View across the transept. FACING PAGE: Detail from a picture of the opening ceremony by H. C. Selous. (The Chinese dignitary pictured among the Diplomatic Corps was in fact the skipper of a Chinese junk, who was 'accidentally' caught up into the ceremonial.)

Meanwhile, the monarch had also become a mother. Four sons and five daughters were born between 1840 and 1857, and the royal residence became the scene of a bustling family life, which provided for the nation an example which could not have been more different from that set by the Queen's royal predecessors.

In domestic matters as in others, the prevailing note in Queen Victoria's attitude was one of commonsense. She had no hesitation in accepting the assistance of medical science as it slowly developed—at the birth of Prince Leopold in 1853 she made moderate use of chloroform for the first time, a pioneering enterprise which did much to render the practice of anaesthesia respectable. She refused to pay lip-service to conventional Victorian attitudes regarding children and marriage. Small babies she found 'froglike', and said of children in general "I can't bear their being idolised & made too gt objects of— or having a number of them about me making a gt noise". In fact, she de-

clared "I am equally shy of marriages & large families . . . better a 1000 times never marry, than marry for marry-ing's sake, wh I believe the gter number of people do". Of course, one must not be misled by strong expres-sions of opinion taken out of context; the Queen was a devoted wife and mother—few can ever have been more so. But she saw with a candour that was not common in her time that such happy marriages and happy families as hers were by no means the universal state of affairs. (It was the

Continued on page 19

The Crimean War of 1854–6 saw a tremendous outburst of patriotic enthusiasm, on the part of the country, the army, and, not least, the Queen herself.

ABOVE: *Soldiers of the Scots Fusilier Guards cheering at Buckingham Palace before departing for the seat of war.*
LEFT: *The Victoria Cross was instituted in 1856, as an award for bravery in the field, and remains the supreme honour of its kind. The first soldier to win it was Sgt. Luke O'Connor, of the Royal Welch Fusiliers, for his gallantry at the battle of the Alma, 1854. Despite being wounded in the shoulder, Sergeant O'Connor recovered the colours from Ensign Anstruther, who had been killed. He carried them throughout the battle, even though the colours were pierced by twenty-six bullets and the shaft almost shot away.*

FACING PAGE: *The marriage of Edward, Prince of Wales, to Princess Alexandra of Denmark, took place in St. George's Chapel, Windsor, on 5 May 1863. The Queen, still in deep mourning for Prince Albert, witnessed the ceremony from the seclusion of a little private gallery, known as Katherine of Aragon's Closet, above the altar. (Top right hand corner of the painting.)*

same refreshingly no-nonsense attitude that enabled her to laugh heartily at jokes that more prudish members of her entourage considered dreadfully shocking; the famous "We are not amused" related to a story which the Queen considered subversive of naval discipline—a quite different affair!)

Her own children were brought up with a care and forethought that marked a revolution in social attitudes not merely in the royal family but in society as a whole. It is true that over-anxious if understandable concern, on the part of both the Queen and her Consort, for the future of the heir to the throne led to the infliction on the Prince of Wales of a programmed upbringing totally unsuitable to his talents and temperament; but the general rule for the others was moderate and reasonable, by the standards of the time, and always governed by affection.

The story of the Queen's relations with the Prince of Wales is really a chapter on its own. All the complicated emotions of a mother and then a widow, a woman often barely at terms with herself, surged around this rather ordinary eldest son. A disappointment when young, and a scapegoat for his father's death, he became an object of jealousy as he matured, and it was only in late middle age that he began to enjoy anything like the confidence of the Queen.

During the lifetime of the Prince Consort, however, the worst strains and tensions were kept at a distance. While the children were young a lively domesticity was the order of the day, with the royal parents joining their family in games of blind man's buff, or visiting the zoo, or improvising plays and charades, or, when they were very small, just merrily dragging them round the room in a basket! "Children though often a source of anxiety and difficulty are a great blessing and cheer & brighten up life" wrote the Queen, and both halves of the characteristically artless statement have the ring of truth.

Christmas was of course one of the great family occasions—greater now than in earlier periods, since Prince Albert brought over from Germany a number of his native Christmas customs, all of them calculated to increase the cosy jollity and family sentiment of the festival. Most notable among these innovations was the Christmas tree, bedecked with candles and

baubles, and loaded with presents, which were distributed with the elaborate ritual which arises, by very necessary instinct, in any large family situation. The whole business appealed immensely to the English middle classes, who took to it with enthusiasm.

The settings in which these happy scenes were acted out changed somewhat over the years. Buckingham Palace was the principal royal residence in the capital where most of the official entertainment took place. Though grand, it was immensely inconvenient, and in the early years of the reign the household fell into a deplorable state of mismanagement. (During the first three months of 1840 dinners were provided at the Palace

for 24,600 persons, many of whom were not in the least entitled to them.) The efforts of Prince Albert substantially reformed the scandals, and the accommodation was gradually improved. However, the formal splendours of this great house in the capital were never well suited to the sort of family life craved by the Queen and her husband.

Windsor Castle provided a more relaxed and rural atmosphere. It was here that the young couple had spent their brief honeymoon; it became the scene of their Christmas festivities and many other family occasions. Here also Prince Albert's improving hand was necessarily in evidence, and among other alterations a system of mains drainage was installed in the

Continued on page 20

1840s; the haphazard sanitation arrangements of centuries in this vast stone honeycomb could not be put right at a stroke, however, and the typhoid which killed the Prince in 1861 found the castle sewers a congenial breeding ground.

Apart from this disastrous defect, Windsor suffered to some degree from the openness to intrusion that made London so unattractive. The public was allowed access to the park and castle with considerable freedom; it was generally felt and admitted to be their right, but sometimes this right was abused, as when in 1849 a group of visitors purloined a royal sketchbook from the slopes and published its contents, offering facsimiles of the royal signature for sale. It was a very deeply-rooted instinct with Queen Victoria to seek privacy, not so as to be absolutely alone, but for the sake of quietness and simplicity in a domestic circle. In this she was unlike most of her immediate forebears, who had revelled in their majesty. It was sad but inevitable that each successive attempt to find a secret retreat was overtaken by the courtly requirements of scale and formality.

The first of these escapes took her to Osborne, on the Isle of Wight. The modest house and estate were purchased in 1844 for £26,000, and the family holidayed there deliciously that same year in their "dear little Home"—"all our *very own*", as the Queen confided to her journal, a phrase that will strike a chord from anyone who has once been young and married and embarked on making a home. But it was not big enough, and the Prince saw scope for improvement, so in 1845 it was pulled down and rebuilt, to become the grand Italianate villa that it still is today. Even after this change in scale, however, it remained very much a private and personal dwelling, stamped with the intimate touch of the young couple who supervised every detail of its making, and whose initials entwine lovingly all over the decorations. Parts of it are extraordinarily untouched by the passage of time, preserved first by the Queen (Prince Albert's watch case still hangs over his side of the bed) and then by her successors.

A taste for isolation, as opposed to mere privacy, and for wild grandeur rather than rustic charm, came a little later. It was in 1848 that the Queen purchased Balmoral in the eastern Highlands of Scotland—"a pretty little Castle in the old scotch style". This marked the beginning of a long and ever-deepening attachment to Scotland, and particularly to the Highlands. The picturesque romance of kilts and bagpipes, lochs and mountains, was a source of fascination to the Queen's highly-strung imagination. But more important still was the almost primitive simplicity of life in the Highlands. The inhabitants lived in conditions of ancient austerity, and the Queen was convinced that their characters were the better for it—

*

LEFT: *The Albert Memorial Chapel at Windsor. The Prince was buried in a splendid mausoleum at Frogmore, where eventually the Queen was laid by his side; but she commemorated his life in a multitude of memorials.*

FACING PAGE: *The luxury of empire. The British in India sometimes lived in splendid style; but, though eastern commerce was prized, imperialism was by no means popular with people at home until the last years of Victoria's reign.*

"I like talking to the people here, they are so simple and straightforward." Life at the castle was not entirely lacking in the amenities of civilisation, but it was undoubtedly cramped to a high degree (so that in the early days, for instance, the Queen would interview a minister-in-attendance perched on the edge of his bed for lack of anywhere else to sit), and it was all part of the fun of staying there that one should enjoy the singularly makeshift quality of the arrangements. Here too rebuilding had to come, in 1853, but this remained the most private of all the royal residences, and after Prince Albert's death the Queen took to spending longer and longer there, so that the summer holidays dragged on far into the autumn, and London, to its mounting discontent, saw her hardly at all.

The turning point in the story of Queen Victoria's whole life comes, of course, in 1861. Prince Albert's health began to deteriorate from about 1858; pulled down by overwork, he never possessed his wife's fighting disposition, and was always prone to psychosomatic illnesses. At the end of 1861 he was much depressed, for a variety of reasons, chief among which was the behaviour of the Prince of Wales, who was sowing his wild oats. When typhoid struck, in late November, it found him an easy victim, and he died after a harrowing illness on Saturday 14 December.

The blow was shattering. Extravagant and prolonged mourning was accepted and expected by the conventions of the time, but Queen Victoria disappeared into almost total seclusion until 1866, and hardly resumed 'normal' life until the late 1870s. The sympathy which this prolonged grief evoked from the nation at the beginning turned slowly into impatience at what came to be regarded as self-indulgence, and finally into resentment at the Queen's failure to perform any of her public duties, while at the same time preventing the Prince of Wales from substituting for her in any but the least important matters.

Much of this criticism was not entirely appropriate, on at least two grounds. First, although the Queen shrank from the public gaze she never ceased to cope in private with the stream of state affairs, carrying out to the letter the scheme of work which she and the Prince had devised

together. Certainly, her ministers frequently found her difficult, and occasionally inaccessible—her duty was a somewhat eccentric conception of her own at these times, but she always strove to carry it out, at a physical and mental cost that was often really severe. Second, it is at least possible, in the view of one recent biographer, that the appalling shock of the Prince Consort's death effected a distinct and quite longlasting physiological change, which caused her neurotic behaviour during this period. Attempts to make her 'snap out of it' produced, as might be expected, a worsening of the condition; a violent attack on her seclusion in 1871 seems to have contributed to a mysterious but genuinely serious illness in August and September during which at one point her physician thought she might have only twenty-four hours to live.

Eventually she found her balance again, and in fact learnt to do something which she had never achieved before during her adult life—to stand on her own, without the assistance of

any male figure to comfort and support her. In the ensuing period of full maturity she was to achieve the formidable status of true greatness.

Before that Indian summer could come, though, there were long and bitter years to pass, of which the most notable feature in terms of the Queen's life as monarch was her complex, shifting, triangular relationship with the two political giants of her era—W. E. Gladstone and Benjamin Disraeli.

Queen Victoria was not neutral or indifferent to any of the ten men who served as Prime Ministers during her reign; indeed, she would have considered it neglect of her duty if she had been. But though her likes and dislikes were often strong, they were generally open to modification, and this modification mostly worked in favour of the minister on closer acquaintance. Thus, although Sir Robert Peel incurred violent hostility when he seemed about to turn out the adored Lord Melbourne, he had by 1843 so risen in the Queen's estimation that she described him in a letter

Continued on page 22

to the King of the Belgians as "a great statesman", while after his tragic death in 1850 she lamented "*he* could less be spared than any other human being". Lords Palmerston and Russell —"those two dreadful old men" as the Queen called them—perhaps did not improve on acquaintance to the same extent; but even they collected some retrospective flowers.

In the cases of Gladstone and Disraeli, matters were complicated first by the virulent and exceptional personal hostility between the two men themselves, and secondly by the magnitude of the political issues and changes which were under discussion during the period of their importance. Even in the privacy of her mourning, the Queen could not help being em-broiled in the bitter struggle between these two titanic figures, and after Disraeli's death in 1881 left the stage clear for Gladstone alone, the increasingly melodramatic story of the Grand Old Man's later career, centring round his attempts to solve the vicious Irish problem, provoked the same violent reactions in the monarch as in the country at large.

Disraeli once explained his success with the Queen in a famous phrase, when he said "Gladstone treats the Queen like a public department; I treat her like a woman". Like many of his epigrams, this hid a deep truth under its over-simple exterior. At first glance one might have expected Queen Victoria to have been attracted by Gladstone's rigid virtue, his sense of duty, his desire to improve mankind in accordance with God's will, more than by Disraeli's exotic, bizarre, seemingly cynical and unprincipled adventurousness. But the woman needed admiration, the widow needed subtle sympathy, the shaken ruler needed reassurance, and Disraeli, not Gladstone, was able to give all these things with a sincerity that was not in the least diminished by the language in which they were clothed—language which both sides recognised for the delightfully light-hearted extravagance that it really was. Moreover, Disraeli's government pursued policies of which the Queen heartily approved, whereas Gladstone, to fevered imaginations at least, seemed intent on dismantling the established structure of the Church, the state, and society itself. Thus Disraeli was gradually able to draw the Queen out of her retirement; Gladstone, on the other hand, drove her on occasion to talk furiously of abdication.

The most important of the Disraelian policies, from the royal point of view, was that which aimed at strengthening Britain's position in the world, consolidating peace in Europe and expanding the empire overseas. Inherited and amplified by successive Conservative governments under Lord Salisbury, this raised British power to a height never attained before, and with it the prestige and glory of the Crown. On May Day 1876 Queen Victoria was proclaimed Empress of India, a new title of which the overtones of grandeur at first caused some critical mutterings at home, but which quickly came to seem a natural part of the monarch's position at the head of an empire which seemed to grow greater year by year, as if by divine decree. There were checks and occasional reverses, but over the years the tide rolled on, until the Queen's Diamond Jubilee of 1897 appeared to be almost her deification as goddess of the imperial ideal. "No-one ever, I believe, has met with such an ovation as was given to me, passing through those six miles of streets . . ." And why? Her people knew:

'Walk wide o' the Widow at Windsor,
For 'alf o' Creation she owns . . .'

To the Queen, this growth was as much a matter of responsibility as of pride; like Kipling when he wrote 'Take up the white man's burden . . .', there was no trace of hypocrisy in her belief that the function of empire was

"NEW CROWNS FOR OLD ONES!"

(ALADDIN adapted.)

"to protect the poor natives and advance civilisation".

Nonetheless, the enthusiasm for empire grew easily, in Queen Victoria's case at least, out of her early and lasting feelings of sympathy for the men of her armed forces—for, after all, this was an empire of conquest, and in the last quarter of the nineteenth century Britain became more of a military nation than had perhaps ever been the case in her history. Though too warmhearted and conscious of human suffering to be bloodthirsty (she paused in the middle of skating festivities at frostbound Osborne in 1870 to recollect the sufferings that the cold must be causing to the wounded on the battlefields of the Franco-Prussian War; and in 1855 she had rebuked the warlike aspirations of King Victor Emmanuel of Sardinia by declaring that kings would have to answer before God for the lives of men whom they caused to die in battle), she was emphatically both a soldier's daughter and a patriot. The Crimean War in particular roused her to identify herself excitedly with the gallantry and sufferings of her troops, as if, she wrote, "they were my own children". She bade emotional farewells to the troops as they departed for the seat of war, and greeted returning veterans with even more feeling, commiserating them on their wounds and presenting medals for good service. "Many of the Privates smiled, others hardly dared look up . . . all touched

*

FACING PAGE: *Not everyone was pleased by the title 'Empress of India', which the Queen acquired by the Royal Titles Act of 1876. This* Punch *cartoon suggests that she was allowing Disraeli to substitute something Orientally dubious in place of decent British royalty.*

ABOVE: *Benjamin Disraeli, who became Earl of Beaconsfield in 1876, was the favourite Prime Minister of Queen Victoria's later life. His carefully cultivated air of mystery and romance undoubtedly contributed to his success; but his tact and skill as a politician were more powerful recommendations.*

RIGHT: *William Ewart Gladstone was Disraeli's bitter rival. The intensely controversial political activity of his later life alarmed the Queen so much that she concluded he was "really wicked" as well as "half crazy". Yet he was devoted in his loyalty to her.*

my hand, the 1st time that a simple Private has touched the hand of his Sovereign . . . I am proud of it—proud of this tie which links the lowly brave to his Sovereign."

The later wars of imperialism evoked similar reactions in their turn. The Queen followed passionately the doings of her troops among Egyptian sands, South African veldt, or Afghan mountain passes, and was always more prepared to express opinions to her ministers on peace and war than on any other single topic. The abandonment (as she saw it) of General Gordon at Khartoum was one of the blackest counts in the Queen's indictment of Gladstone, and she was jealous in preserving what she considered her inalienable right to communicate direct with generals in the field: "The Queen always *has* telegraphed direct to her Generals, and *always* will do so, as they value *that* and *don't* care near so much for a mere official message . . . The Queen *has* the *right* to telegraph congratulations and enquiries to *any one*, and won't stand dictation. She *won't* be a *machine*."

The same imperious will came resolutely into action to rally morale in the Boer War crisis of Black Week, in December 1899. Mr. Balfour, visiting Windsor Castle full of the woeful news from the battlefront in South Africa, was put in his place with appalling firmness: "Please understand that there is no one depressed in this house; we are not interested in the possibilities of defeat; they do not exist." The little old lady before whom the great Prince Bismarck, that man of blood and iron, had sweated with cold fear when they met in 1888, might have been made of tempered steel for all the effect that panic had on her. She faced national disaster with the same imperturbable determination that she showed in the face of the maniacs and would-be assassins who plagued her over the years.

In the last two decades of the nineteenth century the Queen was not merely a national figure. She was by now related to all the royal families of Europe, and the indomitable will that stiffened her ministers' resolve was allied to her positively matriarchal authority in order to compose the eternal squabblings and bickerings of the last generation of European dynasts. Sometimes family affairs lapped over into international politics, and then the correspondence and the meetings with her grandson the

Continued on page 24
23

ABOVE: *Four generations. The christening of Edward, later Duke of Windsor, son of the Duke of York, and grandson of the Prince of Wales.*

*

Emperor of Germany and her granddaughter's husband the Czar of Russia assumed more than private significance.

The new, brash power of Germany was the principal menace to peace in Europe, and the histrionics of Wilhelm II ensured a series of alarums and excursions throughout the 1890s. But the Queen's strength was her calmness. At the time of the Kruger telegram in 1896, when feelings were running high, she maintained firm control, commenting in reply to her son's indignant request that she administer 'a good snub' to the Kaiser, "Those sharp, cutting answers and remarks only irritate and do harm, and in Sovereigns and Princes should be most carefully guarded against. William's faults come from impetuousness (as well as conceit); and calmness and firmness are the most powerful weapons in such cases."

This well-poised balance was entirely characteristic of her full maturity. Throughout her life, indeed, the Queen was a person in whom opposite qualities abounded, but only towards the end did they become reconciled in equilibrium. Thus her imperiousness was matched by a surprising and genuine humility, and her overwhelming dignity by painful shyness. "Unselfish and inconsiderate, tactful and blunt, sympathetic and hard, patient and fidgety, direct and devious, irresistibly charming and bristling with 'repellent power'"—so Lady Longford outlines her contrariety. But mellowness came with years, especially when surrounded by the grandchildren whom she adored and who adored her with a complete lack of the trepidation which so easily gripped their parents in the royal presence.

Her experience contributed as much as her temperament to the final weight of Queen Victoria's wisdom. In 1896 she became the longest-reigning of English sovereigns, as well as the one who had seen most change. Adaptable to the last, she showed as much interest in the first telephones and cinematographic cameras as she had in the first railway trains. Disruption, as opposed to improvement, she always disliked however; and the long-established routines of her life were maintained as the fires of her strength gradually died down.

Her last weeks were spent at Osborne, the home that her husband had built for her. There, in December of 1900 and January of 1901, her health failed, undramatically but quite quickly. Lord Roberts, returning in triumph from South Africa, was the last visitor to be received; but on that day also her journal remained unwritten for the first time in 69 years. Her doctors began issuing bulletins about her health on Saturday 19 January, and she died just after half-past six on the evening of Tuesday 22 January 1901, surrounded by children and grandchildren.

The name of her eldest son was the last word spoken by the dying Queen, and the Kaiser's arm supported her at the end—a symbolic illustration of the old Europe of family monarchies of which she had come to be the centre, and which was soon to be no more. Her death marked the passing, not only of a great British sovereign, but of an epoch.

*   *   *

ACKNOWLEDGMENTS Illustrations are acknowledged as follows: Reproduced by Gracious permission of Her Majesty The Queen pp i cover, 1, 2, 3, 4, 6, 7 (top), 8, 12, 14, 15, 19; National Portrait Gallery pp iv cover, 9, 11, (centre and left), 23; Victoria and Albert Museum, pp ii cover, 17; Radio Times Hulton Picture Library p 16; Mary Evans Picture Library pp 7 (bottom), 10; S. W. Newbery, Hon. F.I.I.P., F.R.P.S. p 20; National Army Museum p 18 (top); Peter Baker p 18 (bottom); Ardea Photographics p 21; Mansell Collection p 22; Popperfoto p 24.

SBN 85372 172 6